Upcycle Your ACCESSORIES!

by Chelsey Luciow

CAPSTONE PRESS
a capstone imprint

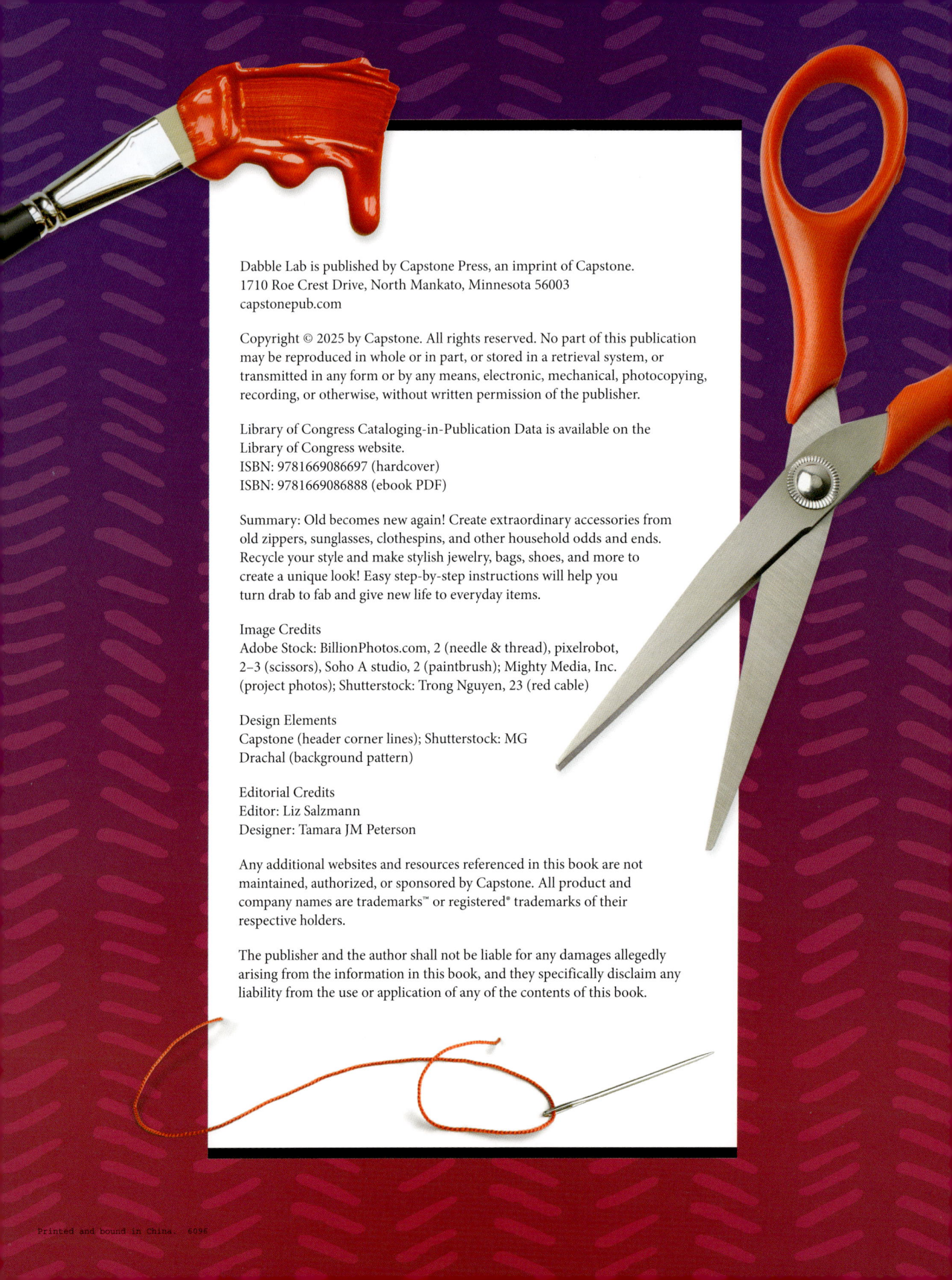

Dabble Lab is published by Capstone Press, an imprint of Capstone.
1710 Roe Crest Drive, North Mankato, Minnesota 56003
capstonepub.com

Copyright © 2025 by Capstone. All rights reserved. No part of this publication may be reproduced in whole or in part, or stored in a retrieval system, or transmitted in any form or by any means, electronic, mechanical, photocopying, recording, or otherwise, without written permission of the publisher.

Library of Congress Cataloging-in-Publication Data is available on the Library of Congress website.
ISBN: 9781669086697 (hardcover)
ISBN: 9781669086888 (ebook PDF)

Summary: Old becomes new again! Create extraordinary accessories from old zippers, sunglasses, clothespins, and other household odds and ends. Recycle your style and make stylish jewelry, bags, shoes, and more to create a unique look! Easy step-by-step instructions will help you turn drab to fab and give new life to everyday items.

Image Credits
Adobe Stock: BillionPhotos.com, 2 (needle & thread), pixelrobot, 2–3 (scissors), Soho A studio, 2 (paintbrush); Mighty Media, Inc. (project photos); Shutterstock: Trong Nguyen, 23 (red cable)

Design Elements
Capstone (header corner lines); Shutterstock: MG Drachal (background pattern)

Editorial Credits
Editor: Liz Salzmann
Designer: Tamara JM Peterson

Any additional websites and resources referenced in this book are not maintained, authorized, or sponsored by Capstone. All product and company names are trademarks™ or registered® trademarks of their respective holders.

The publisher and the author shall not be liable for any damages allegedly arising from the information in this book, and they specifically disclaim any liability from the use or application of any of the contents of this book.

Table of Contents

START YOUR ACCESSORY UPGRADE . . 4
METAL NUT BRACELET. 6
SOUPED-UP SUNGLASSES 8
CLOTHESPIN NECKLACES 10
CREATURE CHARMS. 12
VINTAGE VINYL PURSE 14
BEDAZZLED HEADPHONES 16
PHONE CASE COLLAGES 18
SPRAY-PAINTED BACKPACK. 20
KITTY CORD KEEPERS 22
POCKET PURSE. 24
COMIC COLLAGE SHOES 26
DOG WALKING BOTTLE. 28
GUARD DOG HOLDER 30

Read More 32
Internet Sites 32
About the Author 32

Start Your ACCESSORY Upgrade

Upcycling is when you take something old and change it to make something fresh and new. Accessories are fun and easy to upcycle. With a little creativity, you can turn old backpacks, shoes, headphones, and more into stylish new items to refresh your look!

Basic Supplies

- fabric glue
- hot glue gun
- markers
- needle-nose pliers
- paintbrush
- pencil
- ruler
- scissors
- sewing needle
- super glue
- thread

Crafting Tips

GET READY
Gather all the supplies and read through the instructions carefully before starting a project. Cover your workspace with newspaper or plastic to protect it from messes.

ASK FIRST
Get permission to use any supplies you find.

STAY SAFE
Ask an adult for help using hot or sharp tools.

BE CREATIVE
Project steps are only a guide. Use different materials or try new things to make the project your own!

TIDY UP
Clean your space after you're done crafting. Put supplies back where you found them and wipe down your crafting surface.

METAL NUT BRACELET

Recycled metal nuts make great beads—try braiding some into a bracelet!

WHAT YOU NEED

- paracord
- ruler
- scissors
- cardboard
- metal nuts
- adjustable silicone ring band (or small rubber band)
- lighter (adult help)

Crafting Tip
Try spray-painting the nuts before using them!

1. Cut three 36-inch (91-centimeter) strands of paracord.

2. Tie the three strands together 2 inches (5 cm) from one end.

3. Cut a piece of cardboard approximately 6 by 20 inches (15 by 50 cm). Cut a slit into the top of the cardboard. Slide the knot into the slit.

4. Braid the strands for about 3 inches (7.6 cm).

5. Slide a metal nut onto the left strand.

6. Pass the left strand over the center strand. Slide a metal nut onto the right strand. Pass the right strand over the center strand.

7. Repeat steps 5 and 6 until you have added about 14 metal nuts. Pull the braid tight as you work.

8. Continue braiding the strands until the braid is about 7 inches (18 cm) long. Remove the bracelet from the cardboard.

9. Slide an adjustable silicone ring band onto one strand. Push the band up until it is about ½ inch (1.25 cm) from the end of the braid.

10. Tie the strands in a knot to hold the band in place.

11. Cut the excess paracord off each end near the knots.

12. Have an adult help you seal the ends of the cord by burning the strands with a lighter for a few seconds.

WHAT YOU START WITH

WHAT YOU DO

SOUPED-UP SUNGLASSES

Level up some freebie shades into cool new ones, custom-designed by you!

WHAT YOU NEED

- soap
- water
- towel
- plastic sunglasses
- decorative tape
- acrylic markers
- stickers

1. Clean the glasses with soap and water and dry them off well.

2. Tear off short lengths of decorative tape. Wrap them around the temples of the glasses. Create a design or pattern with the tape.

3. Use acrylic markers to draw simple designs on the frames of the sunglasses.

4. Add stickers to the corners of the frames.

WHAT YOU START WITH

WHAT YOU DO

Crafting Tip

Plan your designs to cover up any logos on the glasses.

CLOTHESPIN NECKLACES

Cute miniatures and clothespins find new life in easy-to-make funky jewelry!

WHAT YOU NEED

- wooden clothespins
- thumbtack
- rubber miniatures
- needle-nose pliers
- ball chain necklaces

10

1. Pull the ends of a clothespin apart to remove the metal spring.

2. Use a thumbtack to poke two holes on opposite sides of a rubber miniature.

3. Use pliers to pull the ends of the metal spring apart. Stick one end into each hole in the miniature.

4. Thread the ball chain necklace through the spring to complete the necklace.

5. Repeat steps 1 through 4 to make more necklaces.

Crafting Tip
This method would also work with large beads instead of rubber miniatures.

WHAT YOU START WITH

WHAT YOU DO

1

2

3

CREATURE CHARMS

Create charming decorations for your backpack using old, small toys!

WHAT YOU NEED

- small plastic or rubber toy animals
- mini screw eye pins
- hair dryer (optional)
- needle-nose pliers
- jump rings
- sequins, beads, or small metal charms (optional)
- key rings

1. Hold a toy animal securely in one hand. Push a screw eye pin into the toy and twist it to the right to screw it in all the way. If it seems too hard, try warming the toy up with a hair dryer, or choose a toy made of a softer material.

2. Use pliers to open a jump ring.

3. If you'd like, put a sequin, bead, or metal charm on the jump ring.

4. Use pliers to close the jump ring around the screw eye pin and key ring.

5. Repeat steps 1 through 4 to make more Creature Charms. Use them for your keys, or attach them to your backpack, purse, or jacket.

WHAT YOU START WITH

WHAT YOU DO

Crafting Tip
Small dog or cat toys would also work for this project!

13

VINTAGE VINYL PURSE

Create a trendy new purse with old vinyl records, an old pair of jeans, and a purse strap.

WHAT YOU NEED

- 2 old vinyl records
- scrap wood
- hammer
- 1/16-inch (1.6-millimeter) nail
- ruler
- old pair of jeans
- scissors
- chalk
- two-part epoxy
- large-eyed needle
- embroidery floss
- heavy metal wire
- needle-nose pliers
- recycled purse strap

14

WHAT YOU START WITH

WHAT YOU DO

1. Set a record on a piece of scrap wood. Use the hammer and nail to make a line of holes halfway around the record. The holes should be ½ inch (1.3 cm) from the edge and spaced ½ inch (1.3 cm) apart.

2. Find the midpoint between the ends of the line of holes. Make a hole there ½ inch (1.3 cm) from the edge of the record.

3. Repeat steps 1 and 2 with the second record.

4. Cut one leg off the jeans. Cut it in half along the seams. Lay one of the halves flat. Use chalk to mark a rectangle that is 6 by 30 inches (15 by 76 cm). Cut out the rectangle.

5. Fold the short edges of the rectangle over ½ inch (1.3 cm). Glue the folds in place with two-part epoxy.

6. Glue a long edge of the rectangle under the edge of a record along the line of holes. Glue the other long edge under the edge of the other record the same way. Let the epoxy cure overnight.

7. Thread the needle with embroidery floss. Tie a knot at the end. Sew through the holes to stitch the fabric to the records.

8. Cut two pieces of wire about 2 inches (5 cm) long. Stick a wire through each of the holes you made in step 2. Use needle-nose pliers to bend the wires into rings.

9. Attach the ends of the purse strap to the rings. Use your vintage vinyl purse to carry your essentials with stylish flair!

15

BEDAZZLED HEADPHONES

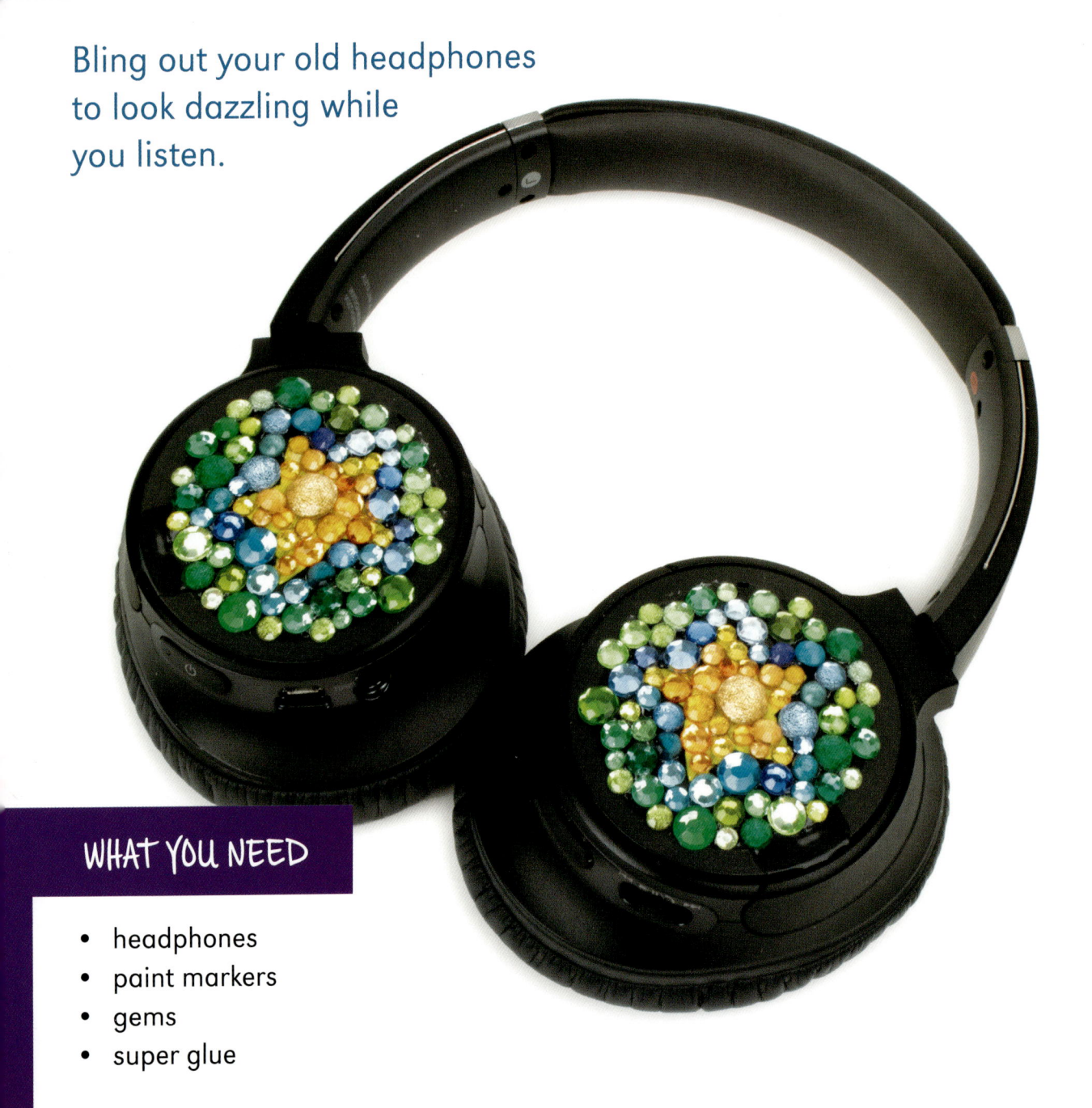

Bling out your old headphones to look dazzling while you listen.

WHAT YOU NEED

- headphones
- paint markers
- gems
- super glue

16

1. Find a flat surface on the headphones that can be covered with gems. Make sure not to cover any holes for sound or cords.

2. Use paint pens to draw shapes, such as stars, on the headphones. Let the paint dry.

3. Fill in the shapes with gems. Working on a small area at a time, glue the gems in place.

4. Fill in the area around the shapes with other colors of gems. Glue the gems in place.

5. Let the glue dry completely before using your bedazzled headphones.

WHAT YOU START WITH

WHAT YOU DO

Crafting Tip
Instead of a central shape, you could draw your initials or an abstract design.

17

PHONE CASE COLLAGES

Easily switch your phone case between different personal designs made with paper scraps, last year's calendar, old magazines, and stickers!

WHAT YOU NEED

- clear plastic phone case
- card stock
- pencil
- scissors
- patterned paper
- glue stick
- magazines, junk mail, and old calendars
- drawing supplies, glitter, or stickers (optional)

18

1. Trace around the phone case on card stock. Cut out the shape. This will be the base for a collage. Cut out a base for each collage you want to make. Be sure to cut a hole where the phone's camera lens is.

2. Choose a patterned paper to be the background of a collage. Trace around a base on the patterned paper and cut out the shape. Glue it to the base.

3. Cut images out of magazines, junk mail, and old calendars.

4. Arrange the images on the background. Trim them to fit on the base. Glue them in place.

5. Draw on designs or add glitter or stickers if you'd like.

6. Repeat steps 2 through 5 for each collage you want to make.

7. Put a collage inside the phone case. Put the case on your phone. Change the collage to match your mood!

WHAT YOU START WITH

WHAT YOU DO

Crafting Tip
Consider making seasonal designs for different holidays!

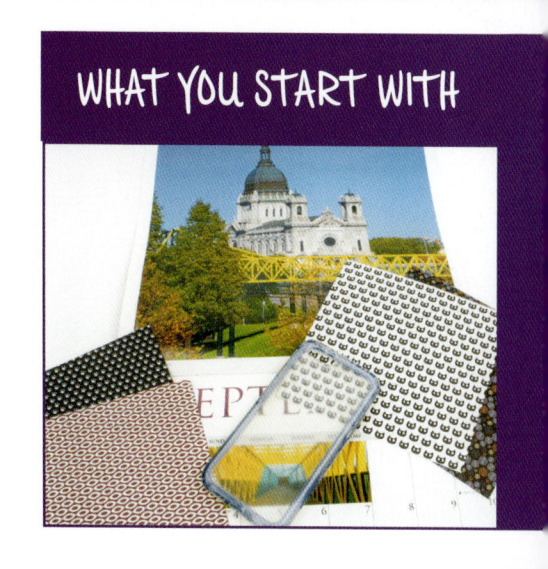

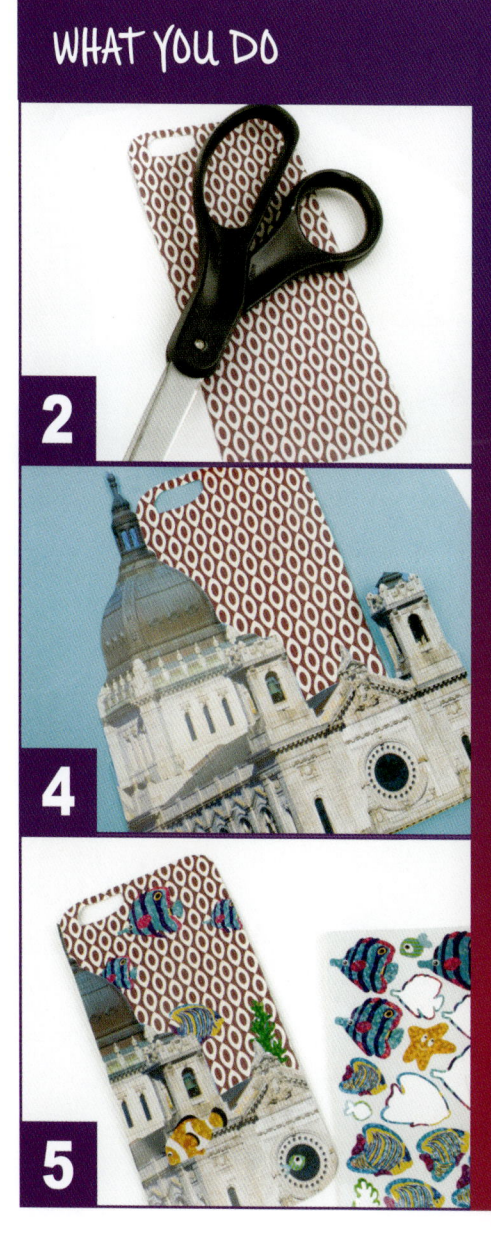

SPRAY-PAINTED BACKPACK

You'll no longer mistake your backpack for your friend's, since no one will have a backpack like yours!

WHAT YOU NEED

- backpack
- masking tape
- spray paint (3 or more colors)
- stickers or paper or foam shapes
- scrap denim
- marker
- scissors
- fabric glue
- paintbrush
- metal studs (optional)

1. Cover the backpack's zippers with masking tape. This will keep the paint off of them.

2. Make sure you work in a well-ventilated space, ideally outside. Spray-paint the front of the backpack with swirls of one paint color. Let the paint dry.

3. Lay stickers or shapes on the bag. Spray-paint over them with a different color. Remove the stickers or shapes. Let the paint dry.

4. Repeat step 3 with different stickers or shapes and a different color of paint. Let the paint dry.

5. Remove the masking tape.

6. Trace or draw a shape, such as a star, on the scrap denim. Cut it out.

7. Cut a rectangle out of the scrap denim. Pull at the edges until they start to fray.

8. Put fabric glue on the lighter side of the rectangle. Glue it to the front of the backpack. Put glue on the darker side of the other denim shape. Glue it on top of the denim rectangle. Let the glue dry.

9. If you'd like to add more detail to the denim shape, attach metal studs.

WHAT YOU START WITH

WHAT YOU DO

Crafting Tip
When you apply fabric glue, use a paintbrush to spread it evenly.

21

KITTY CORD KEEPERS

These kitties made from old leather belts can keep the cord mess all wrapped up!

WHAT YOU NEED

- old leather belts
- scissors
- self-adhesive hook and loop tape
- binder clip
- markers
- super glue
- googly eyes
- jewels
- toothpicks
- paint and paintbrush

22

1. Cut a piece about 6 to 8 inches (15 to 20 cm) long out of the middle of a belt. Be sure it includes the belt's holes.

2. Cut both ends in the shape of cat ears.

3. Cut 2 inches (5 cm) of hook and loop tape. Stick the two sides together. Peel the backing off one side. Stick the tape to the back of the belt piece near one end.

4. Peel the backing off the other side of the tape. Fold the belt piece in half so the ears line up. Press it against the tape.

5. Use a binder clip to keep the belt piece folded overnight. This helps train the leather to stay in the folded position.

6. Use markers, googly eyes, jewels, toothpicks, and paint to add features to the cord keeper.

7. Repeat steps 1 through 6 to make more Kitty Cord Keepers. Use them to keep your computer and phone cords neat and tidy.

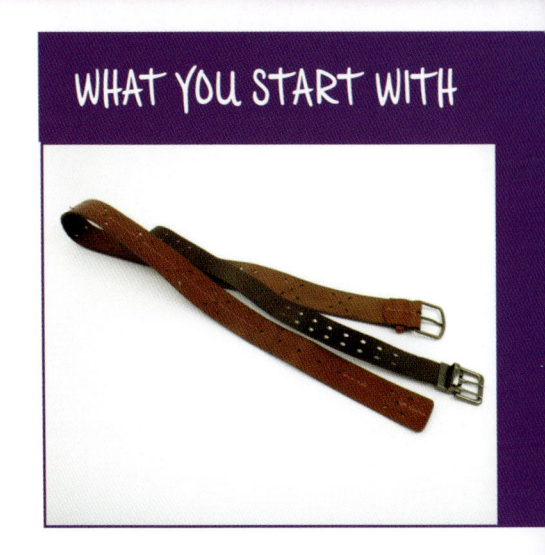

WHAT YOU START WITH

WHAT YOU DO

2

3

5

POCKET PURSE

Make a new denim purse out of your favorite old jeans and a chunky necklace.

WHAT YOU NEED

- old jeans
- scissors
- sewing needle and thread
- chunky chain necklace with a large pendant
- embroidery floss (optional)

1. Cut off the legs of the jeans. Cut each side of the jeans along the seams. Cut along the top, above the top seam.

2. Fold the jeans in half so one back pocket is on each side.

3. Cut along the folded edge. You should now have two matching rectangles with a back pocket in the middle of each.

4. Line up the two rectangles with the pockets facing each other. Use a simple running stitch to sew the side and bottom edges together.

5. Fold the top edges over and sew them in place.

6. Turn the purse right side out. Stick a finger into the two bottom corners to push the corners out.

7. Remove the pendant from the necklace. Sew one end of the necklace to each top corner of the purse. Use 5 to 8 stitches for each end to ensure durability.

8. Sew the pendant to the purse for a finishing touch.

WHAT YOU START WITH

WHAT YOU DO

Crafting Tip
Use embroidery floss to decorate the pockets for added flair.

25

COMIC COLLAGE SHOES

WHAT YOU NEED

- canvas shoes
- paper for stuffing shoes
- comics page (or other decorative paper)
- pencil
- scissors
- Mod Podge
- paintbrush
- clear acrylic spray (optional)

Yeow! Check out these shoes made with a collage of recycled comics!

26

1. Remove the laces from the shoes. Stuff the shoes with paper.

2. Place a scrap of a comics page on a shoe. Use a pencil to trace the seams of the shoe onto the comics page.

3. Cut out the shape you traced on the comics page. Brush Mod Podge onto the back of the paper and the shoe. Carefully press the paper into place and smooth it down.

4. Continue to cut pieces of paper to cover the rest of the section and glue them in place with Mod Podge. It's okay for the pieces to overlap.

5. Repeat steps 2 through 4 to cover the other shoe with comics.

6. Let the Mod Podge dry. Then brush another layer of Mod Podge over the comics on both shoes. Let the Mod Podge dry completely before wearing the shoes.

WHAT YOU START WITH

WHAT YOU DO

Crafting Tip
To make the paper more durable, spray the shoes with a clear acrylic spray.

DOG WALKING BOTTLE

Stay prepared with on-the-go dog bags hidden in an old medicine bottle!

WHAT YOU NEED

- keychain clip
- rope or paracord
- ruler
- medicine bottle with lid
- rubber band
- hot glue gun
- scissors
- bags

1. Thread the keychain clip onto the rope about 5 inches (12.7 cm) from the end.

2. Fold the rope at the keychain clip and attach it to the bottle with a rubber band.

3. Wrap the short end of the rope under the bottom of the bottle and hot glue it to the other side.

4. Wrap the long end of the rope around the bottle starting at the bottom. Apply hot glue every few inches to hold the rope in place. Each time, let the glue dry for 30 to 60 seconds before continuing to wrap the rope.

5. When you reach the lip of the bottle, cut the rope so the end is behind the loop with the hook. Hot glue the end in place.

6. Glue rope around the bottle's lid starting at the bottom. When you get to the top, wrap the rope in a tight spiral. Cut the rope and glue the end to the center of the lid. Let the glue dry.

7. Pack the bottle with bags and clip it to your dog's leash.

WHAT YOU START WITH

WHAT YOU DO

Crafting Tip
This bottle could also hold small items such as lip balm or coins!

GUARD DOG HOLDER

Keep your accessories safe with this organizer made from an old paper tray!

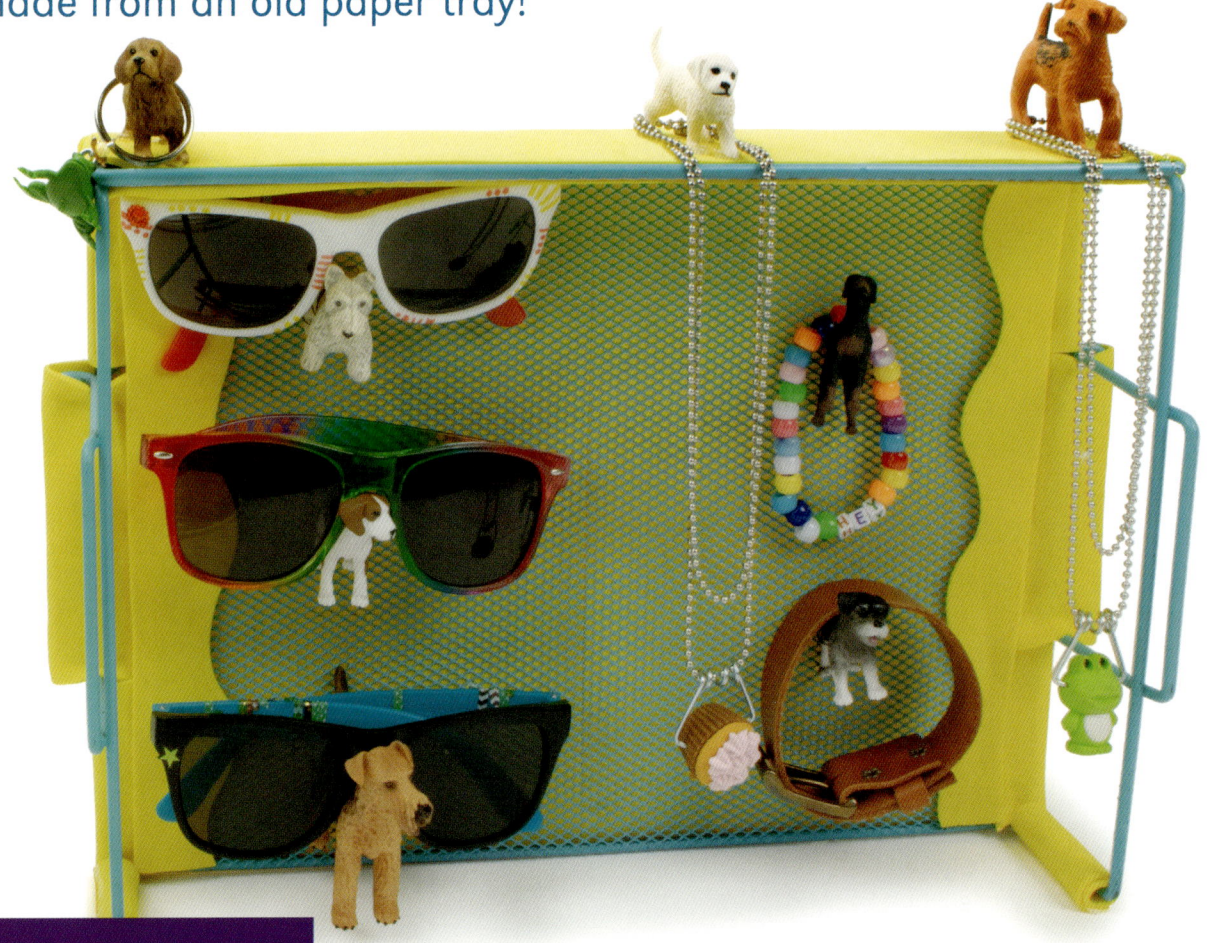

WHAT YOU NEED

- metal paper tray with holes
- spray paint
- small toy dogs or other animals
- accessories
- marker
- wire and wire cutter
- ruler
- craft foam
- scissors
- hot glue gun

30

1. Take the tray outside or to a well-ventilated room. Spray-paint it. Let the paint dry.

2. Arrange the toys and accessories on the tray. Mark the tray where each toy goes.

3. Cut a piece of wire about 2 feet (0.6 meters) long. Wrap the middle of the wire around a toy. Push the ends of the wire through the tray where the toy should go. Twist the ends of the wire together behind the tray.

4. Push the ends back through to the front and wrap them around the toy again to make it extra secure. Push the ends to the back again. Twist them together and cut off any extra wire.

5. Repeat steps 3 and 4 to attach the other toys to the tray.

6. Set the tray on two sheets of craft foam. Make cuts in the foam at the corners of the tray so you can wrap the foam around the edges and top of the tray. Hot glue the craft foam to the tray.

7. Cut wavy borders out of craft foam. Hot glue them to the sides of the tray. Cut strips of craft foam and wrap them around the edges that the tray will rest on.

8. Hot glue a few toys to the top of the tray to hold more accessories.

9. Hang your accessories on their hooks!

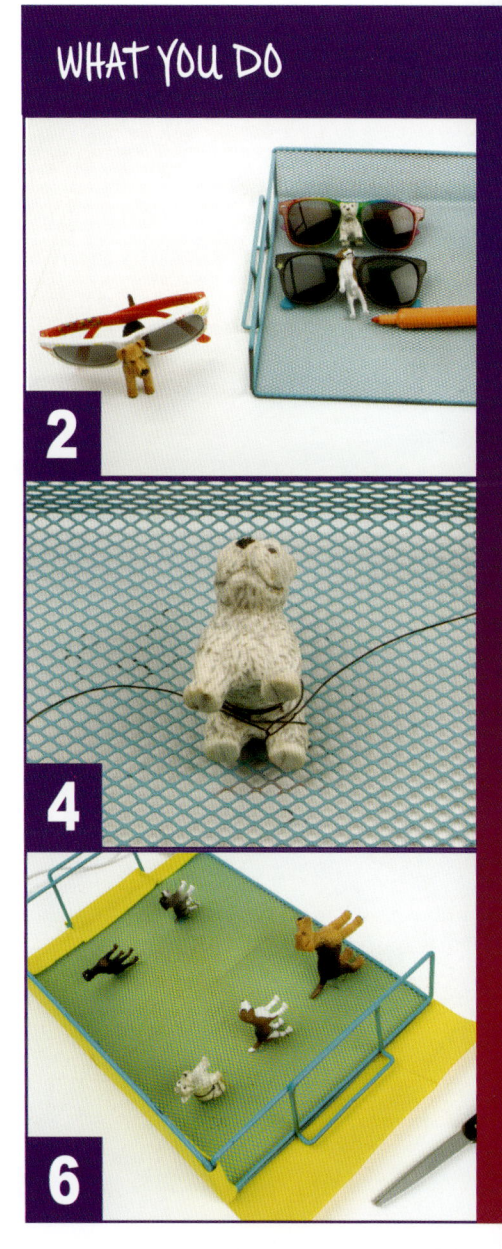

WHAT YOU START WITH

WHAT YOU DO

Read More

Corfee, Stephanie. *Craft Lab for Kids: 52 DIY Projects to Inspire, Excite, and Empower Kids to Create Useful, Beautiful Handmade Goods*. Beverly, MA: Quarry Books, 2020.

Knots, Masha. *The Beginner's Guide to Friendship Bracelets: Essential Lessons for Creating Stylish Designs to Wear and Give*. San Rafael, CA: Rocky Nook Inc., 2022.

Internet Sites

40+ Best Kids' Craft Ideas
positivelysplendid.com/kids-craft-ideas/

16 Gorgeous DIY Necklace Crafts for Kids to Make
justbrightideas.com/diy-necklace-crafts-for-kids/

60+ Fun Crafts for Tweens and Teens
funlovingfamilies.com/crafts-for-tweens-and-teens/

About the Author

Chelsey Luciow is an artist and creator. She loves reading with kids and believes books are magical. Chelsey lives in Minneapolis with her wife, their son, and their dogs.